Forever Facing South

THE STORY OF THE S.S. PALO ALTO, "THE OLD CEMENT SHIP" OF SEACLIFF BEACH

1981

Forever Facing South

THE STORY OF THE S.S. PALO ALTO, "THE OLD CEMENT SHIP" OF SEACLIFF BEACH

DAVID W. HERON

OTTER B BOOKS
1991

To Winifred

Contents

Foreword

I was first introduced to the *Palo Alto* by Louie Guerra, a childhood fishing partner, and his Uncle Paulie. We would drive over from Hollister in Paulie's old red Chevrolet pickup, and while he stood watch on the upper deck on the lookout for the park rangers, Louis and I would scramble down into the ship through the big crack in its center. Standing on the slippery compartment floor which was exposed at low tide, we snagged huge rubber-mouth perch with wicked treble hooks the size of our fists.

I can still remember the metallic taste of the fear caused by doing something not only dangerous but very illegal, and I remember even more vividly the sounds that the ship made as the water washed in and out of the compartments, forcing the air to moan through portholes, hatches, and cracks. I spent many exciting hours clambering through the ship and I became convinced that the creaks and groans meant that the spirit of the ship was still alive, and the sounds were sighs of sadness — a lament for a life never lived.

The *Palo Alto*, built by the San Francisco Shipbuilding Company at Alameda just after the end of World War I, evolved from a wartime effort to find alternatives to iron and steel ships. (I would have loved to have been at the meeting where the designer tried to sell the committee on *that* idea.) Designed with a honeycomb of oil compartments, dry cargo compartments, and dead air spaces separated by concrete walls, the ship was supposed to float even if broken in two. Her designer never said anything about what would happen if she was broken in two after she sank, but her unique design has contributed to her ability to withstand the constant pounding of the sea. When you consider all the sea walls, rip-rap, piers, wharves, and breakwaters that the ocean has eaten along this coast over the years, the *Palo Alto* is certainly a tough old bird.

It was a sad day in January 1930 when the captain assigned to her when she was originally commissioned stood at attention as the ship settled to the sea floor at Seacliff. With tears streaming down his face, he patted her side one last time and left her to her fate of forever plowing through the sea but always standing still.

Dave Heron's history of the *Palo Alto* brings all the elements of the fascinating story together: the evolution of concrete shipbuilding; the United States Shipping Board's belated decision to try it; the remarkable story of Leslie Comyn and the San Francisco Shipbuilding Company; the sad, final journey from the mudflats of San Francisco Bay to the shining strand at Seacliff; and her final career as The Concrete Ship.

Heron's history is a timely tribute to an old friend. It may just be the tricks played by memory, but the fish seem smaller these days, and the ship seems to have shrunk from her original length of 435 feet. The concrete surface is worn away in many places, exposing the spaghetti of reinforcing bars, and she is now not only broken, but also out of plumb, like a badly broken nose. But, considering the hammering she has taken from Pacific storms, she wears her seventy years well. Hunkered down in the sand with her backside braced against the beach, her spine broken and twisted and her ribs poking through her skin, the *Palo Alto* faces with dignity the role that fate has dealt her.

Sandy Lydon
Aptos, California
May, 1991

Introduction

March and April in Reno have bright and beautiful ski weather, but to a native of the coastal lowlands it's a long wait for spring to turn the Truckee Meadows green. A March trip to San Francisco from the eastern Sierra is a jump from winter into spring, from dark and dormant to green and efflorescent.

So when neighbors offered to lend us their trailer, we bundled year-old Charlie in the back of the car and headed for the coast. I seemed to remember that there was trailer camping on the beach at Seacliff, and thinking about the sound and smell of the surf promised a welcome contrast to the brown chill of early spring in the Great Basin.

After an easy trip from brown to green over the mountains and across the San Joaquin Valley, a prayerful drive down the teeming Nimitz Freeway and another through the redwoods of Highway 17, we got to Seacliff just after sundown. It was mid-week, and there were several camping spots to choose from. (These days, even for weekdays you make your computer reservations a month in advance, and may find yourself on a waiting list.)

With a baby aboard we settled close to the restrooms, which also had a phone, so we could see how teenage son Jim was surviving by himself back at home.

I backed the trailer into its parking spot, hooked up the lights and the hose, and we began our introduction to camping with a "rig". Between us and the restrooms was an Airstream, a thirty-foot ovoid of polished aluminum belonging to a friendly couple from Southern California. On the other side was a collapsible tent-trailer belonging to a young Swiss chef from San Francisco, his wife, and their six-year-old son.

We toasted the sunset and put Charlie in a backpack for his first close view of the ocean and a walk along the hard wet sand at low tide. Monterey Bay was calm, the surf gentle, and the evening air was moist and heavy with the fragrance of the sea.

We turned east along the shore, and for the first time I noticed the pier, and at the end of it the old ship, lying low in the water. As we approached, I could see a break in the hull on the starboard side, forward of what remained of the cabin deck. The bow seemed to have settled into the sand. We walked under the pier, and were close enough to see, on the curved stern of the ship, below where the rudder shaft had been, the lines left by wooden forms.

The old ship was built of concrete!

The year was 1966. Although I didn't know it, three years before, heavy seas had broken the hull, where the bow hung out

Charlie Heron enjoying Seacliff Beach, spring 1966.

First glimpse of pier and Palo Alto, *with hamburger stand at lee end of pier.*

beyond the sandstone shelf, where a crack had appeared in the winter of 1932. For the last three years the winter storms had been gentle. The retaining wall along the beach, the pier, and the ship had for the moment been spared the pummeling they were to receive a few years later.

How had this big concrete ship come to be sitting here on the beach on the shore of Monterey Bay? Where and when had she been built? What ports had she seen on her voyages around the world? What cargoes had she carried? What was her name and registry?

The next morning after breakfast and a conversation with the Airstream people Winnie gave Charlie a bath in his little plastic tub on the picnic table and I headed for the pier.

At the leeward end of the wharf stood a bait and hamburger stand, the proprietor just lifting the plywood window-covers. (The same building now stands back against the bluff across the road from the pier.)

There were already fishermen out on the old ship and more on the way out across the heavy redwood planks of the wharf.

I stopped at the bait shop and asked the man who was setting out fishing poles if he knew the name of the ship.

"*Palo Alto*" he said, "She was built by the Navy in the First World War, and towed here during the Depression."

I thanked him, and continued out toward the *Palo Alto*. The wheel house at the stern (which I later learned had been Ralph Creffield's boat and bait shop in the late forties and fifties) was still standing, but the doors were boarded up. The concrete of the deck was showing signs of wear; here and there the reinforcing bars showed through. In front of the wheel house was a sturdy iron step structure which had held the aft mast. Through a hole in an old hatch cover amidships air moaned in and out as water rose and fell down in the hold. The concrete and cable railings were lined with fishermen. Amidships the remains of the cabin structure held a high chain link fence to keep people back from the break in the hull.

She was a sad old relic of a ship, but she had obviously endured for a number of years, and hosted more happy people sitting there on the beach than most steamships of her age.

Back at the trailer we were visited by a ranger, come to collect our three dollar camping fee. I asked him if he knew the history of the *Palo Alto*.

A little, he said. She had been been towed to Seacliff in 1930, before the beach had become a state park, and had been a dance hall and restaurant. The state had bought her when it bought the beach, and maintained her as a fishing pier. He thought she had been built by the Navy as an oil tanker, but didn't know when or where. (His mention of the Navy was one of the many apocrypha surrounding the old ship; I have quoted others, trying to identify them as misinformation.)

Some day, I said to myself, I'd like to know the story of the *Palo Alto*.

Twenty years later, after I retired as a librarian, the search began. First, I visited the National Archives Records Center at San Bruno, and with the help of the archivists there and in Washington, discovered Record Group 32, the papers of the United States Shipping Board Emergency Fleet Corporation. The National Maritime Museum's library at Fort Mason in San Francisco provided good photographs and history of World War I shipbuilding, the Stanford University and University of California libraries provided old government reports, books and contemporary articles about concrete ships.

That was the beginning. From these sources, from endless blinding hours of newspapers on film, from the Aptos Library's clipping file, and from records of the State Park Service and Santa Cruz County, the story of the old ship has emerged. There are some blank spots, and some apocryphal inventions which (suitably acknowledged) seemed worth repeating. Although the *Palo Alto's* story had moments of excitement, a lot of the time between her launching in May of 1919 to her most recent reopening in 1986 was spent just sitting in Benicia, in Oakland, and on the beach at Seacliff, looking the best she could, given the ravages of time and tide.

Even during these quiet times things have happened which should be a part of her chronicle, but are not. The story is by no means complete, and I hope that recording what I have found will bring more pictures, anecdotes, and relics to the Seacliff Visitors' Center, and give visitors some answers to the riddle of the old cement ship.

I must acknowledge with gratitude the help which I have received from the National Archives, particularly from Robert E. Richardson of the Cartographic and Architectural Branch and John K. VanDereedt of the Judicial, Fiscal, and Social Division, from Jeanne Thieverge, of the Redwood City Public Library, Sibylle Zemitis, of the California State Library, Irene Stachura of the Maritime Museum Library in San Francisco, marine model builder Tom Fordham, the Pajaro Valley Historical Society, Harold van Gorder, Mrs. Ralph Creffield, and Rose Costa, from Rangers Bob Culbertson, Jack Kirchner, and Chris Sanguino, from Vernon Pike, Barney Levy, and Ranger Jim Fife of the Monterey Bay Natural History Association, from Stanley Stevens, Map Librarian of UCSC, and Bob Smith of the *Watsonville Register-Pajaronian*, and from Heidi Smith and Rose Church of the Aptos Library. Last but not least, many thanks to Sandy Lydon for his encouragement and generous help with photographs and his encyclopedic fund of Central California history.

David W. Heron
Aptos, California
February 1991

Forever Facing South

The Story of the S.S. Palo Alto, "The Old Cement Ship" of Seacliff Beach

First of the Fleet

The sky was overcast on Thursday afternoon, May 29, 1919, and a cool breeze riffled the water of the San Antonio Estuary. The newly-built ceremonial platform, next to the bow of the big concrete hull at the San Francisco Shipbuilding Company's yard on Government Island, was draped in bunting and full of people.

At two fifteen, after the speeches, Anna May Wig shattered a ribboned bottle of champagne against the bow, below where the name *Palo Alto* was inset in the concrete. The stops were released, and the 435 foot ship slid to starboard down the wooden ways into the inner harbor between Oakland and Alameda.

S.S. Palo Alto *just before launching at the SF Shipbuilding Co.'s Yard, Oakland*

4

The moment concrete touches water, May 29, 1919.

Just after launching, she is being towed along the San Antonio Estuary to the "outfit dock".

San Francisco Shipbuilding Company

Superintendent for
United States Shipping Board
Emergency Fleet Corporation
Concrete Ship Section

Cordially invite you to witness

the launching of the

7500 ton Reinforced Concrete Ship

"Palo Alto"

Government Island, Oakland California

Thursday, May twenty-ninth

Nineteen hundred and nineteen

at 2:30 p. m.

Invitation to the launching.

Mrs. Wig had come out from Washington with her husband, Rudolph James Wig, a mechanical engineer and head of the Concrete Ship Section of the U.S. Shipping Board Emergency Fleet Corporation, to officiate at the launching of the new tanker. Wig sent a wire to Washington that evening from Oakland reporting the event to Board President Edward N. Hurley.

It was an event of some importance to the San Francisco Bay waterfront. Crowds on the shore cheered and waved, and boats and nearby factories blew their whistles as the *Palo Alto* settled into the estuary. With the Wigs, other USSB officials, and officers of the shipbuilding company on the christening platform were the mayors of Oakland, Alameda, and Berkeley, as well as representatives of Alameda County, the Oakland Chamber of Commerce, the Merchants' Exchange, and Bay area newspapers.

Aside from the fact that she was built of reinforced concrete, the launching of the *Palo Alto* was remarkable for two reasons. The hull had been finished in a record 120 days from the first pouring, on the 20th of January. The actual pouring had taken only two weeks (the rest of the time required for curing, removing forms, finishing, and painting). But there was another even more important cause for celebration.

In early May 1918 the United States Shipping Board had announced that it would build a fleet of thirty-eight 7500-ton concrete ships. Now, almost exactly a year later, the first of these vessels was actually afloat. As it turned out, only eight were eventually completed, but the *Palo Alto* was first to be launched.

The timing of the Shipping Board's plan to build a large fleet of concrete ships was not ideal. Less than six months later, on November 11, the Armistice was signed. The war in Europe was over; on the day of the launching the Paris Peace Conference was debating German reparations. The War Effort, with its industrial and federal bureaucracy, had been gathering momentum, however, since the U.S. had declared war on Germany in 1917. During the two years from that time to the Armistice, the Emergency Fleet Corporation built a staff of 8,000 and enough inertial force to carry it beyond the end of the emergency.

After naval battles on the Atlantic had ended, the demand for concrete ships disappeared almost as suddenly as the demand for destroyers, cannon, and tanks. The *Palo Alto* cost an estimated $1.5 million. She was a well-built oil tanker, with a 2800 horsepower steam engine, bronze fittings, an eleven ton bronze propeller fifteen feet in diameter, a fifteen ton rudder, decks of white Norwegian ash, and a tile-floored galley. She had fourteen water-tight oil compartments with a total carrying capacity of three million gallons. Today's supertankers hold hundreds of millions, but for her day the *Palo Alto* was a sizeable ship.

Mars, god of war, has never been thrifty; the older he gets the more profligate he becomes; even the First World War was wasteful. The new million-dollar tanker launched so proudly on May 29, 1919 and commissioned in October 1920, lay at anchor, virtually discarded, in Oakland and Benicia for the next four years; when the Shipping Board finally sold her on December 22, 1924, it was at the surplus-scrap price of $18,750.

When the State of California bought her in February 1936, she was lying in the sand on the shore of Monterey Bay. Sixteen years after Anna May Wig splashed champagne on her bow and she slid triumphantly into the Oakland Estuary, the *Palo Alto* was sold for a dollar.

Today the gracefully curved stern of the *Palo Alto* still lies firmly on the beach, but the the hull is broken in several places, listing to starboard amidships, and forward, beyond where the bridge once stood, she has been devoured by the force of the sea. Her sturdy concrete bow, tormented by stormy surf and unsupported by the sandstone shelf, has broken away and half submerged. At high tide the forecastle, white with guano, is a small pelican island separated by fifty feet of swirling water from the rest of the hull. At lowest tides a jumbled mass of steel reinforcing bars, freed of its cement casing, rises out of the sea in a space which was once the forward oil cargo tank.

Even today, thanks to the Seacliff volunteers who gave many hundreds of hours to rebuilding the after deck and the pier in 1983, enough of the *Palo Alto* survives that, standing at the stern and facing forward (which is forever south) along the deck out into Monterey Bay, one can imagine the ship she was, and might have been.

If she had been launched a year earlier, while the U-Boats were still sinking Atlantic shipping, her fate might have been different.

It might have been even more different if, on Friday, November 26 — the day after Thanksgiving — in 1920, a crucial day in the saga of the *Palo Alto*, two New York investors named Martin Spielberg and George Williams had not met Captain Paul Foley, U.S.N., the Emergency Fleet Corporation's Director of Operations, in his Washington office, and asked his professional opinion of concrete ships.

CHAPTER II

Ships Built of Stone

Nicolay Knudtzon Fougner was a young Norwegian civil engineer working in the Philippines in 1910. There he became involved in building a small harbor vessel with a concrete hull, and suddenly discovered his career. Concrete had been used to build small boats as early as the middle of the 19th century. During the first years of the First World War Fougner became convinced that it could be used less expensively than steel to replace ships lost to submarines in the Atlantic. Between 1916 and 1918 he succeeded in building several such vessels in Norway; after these successes, in partnership with his brother Herman, he was able to arouse some interest in the United States.

Among conservative seafarers, however, Fougner's radical ideas were not readily accepted. In 1962 maritime historian Jean Haviland wrote an excellent account of American concrete ships of both world wars (they have been less popular in peacetime). In it she compared mariners' suspicion of cement ships with the way people in Glasgow, used to wooden ships, felt about the first iron steamer built on the Clyde in 1831.

"City folk" she wrote, "warned their relatives from the country on no account to entrust their lives to the new vessel, `as it was weel kent in Glesga that iron couldna soom'... How much more would these people have distrusted a ship built of stone!"

By the time Fougner patented his first stone ship in 1912, steel ships had all but replaced wooden ones. However, four years later the war in Europe had greatly reduced the Allies' stockpiles of steel. Fougner was convinced that the time had come to make serious use of reinforced concrete in shipbuilding. In his book, *Seagoing and Other Concrete Ships*, published in London in 1922 and based "on personal experience gained in the construction of about thirty vessels of concrete in the last five years", Fougner argued that cost, stability, ease of repair, immunity to fire and corrosion, insulation, and cleanliness all favored concrete ships. A 1920 American Concrete Institute report in *Scientific American* said "In service concrete ships stood up quite well. In fact there is generally less vibration in concrete ships than in corresponding steel ships, and also a considerable increase in the period of roll, which is desirable, and is apparently due to the fact that these vessels have a larger moment of inertia around the longitudinal axis than steel ships."

Fougner did concede that steel hulls were lighter, and (with what might be regarded as understatement) that "the shell [of a steel ship] is better able to withstand local blows and scratches resulting from rough handling." There has, of course, never been much doubt that concrete was more brittle than other shipbuilding materials. On the other hand, repairs to concrete hulls were relatively simple and inexpensive.

Fougner's first seagoing ship was the *Namsenfjord*, launched on August 2, 1917, 84 feet long, with a capacity of 200 tons. Because Norway's Department of Shipping regarded it as an experimental vessel, it took four months to issue the permit to build it, and the application had to be reviewed by a technical committee. However Norway, in spite of its neutrality, had lost nearly half its merchant fleet during the war, and at the end of March Fougner got permission to build. Later, with the *Namsenfjord* under construction, he received permits to start two larger vessels, the 600-ton *Stier* and the 1000-ton *Askelad*.

With each of these vessels the Fougners refined their designs, reduced weight, made the hulls more seaworthy, strengthened the critical structure of engine mounting and stern posts, and improved their aggregates and steel reinforcement.

On April 6, 1917, a week after Nicolay Fougner got his permit to build the *Namsenfjord*, the United States declared war on Germany. The following year, through the newly-formed U.S. Shipping Board Emergency Fleet Corporation, the American government began an eight billion dollar construction program to replace ships sunk by the German U-Boat fleet. The U.S. shipbuilding program presented a much larger market than Norway could offer, and Fougner's brother Hermann, who lived in New York, was soon on his way to Washington with plans for sturdy, economical concrete ships to help the Emergency Fleet Corporation through its wartime steel shortage.

Hermann Fougner's claims for stone ships were confirmed by the *Namsenfjord's* successful trials in August, and by October both brothers were in Washington conferring with the Shipping Board. Early in 1918 Rudolph Wig was made Chief Engineer of a new Concrete Ship Section. In early April Wig presented his recommendations to Shipping Board Chairman Edward Hurley, and on April 12 President Woodrow Wilson approved an emergency appropriation to build concrete ships.

One of the first Shipping Board orders for these stone ships was to the Fougner Concrete Shipbuilding Company, which launched the *Polias*, at Flushing Bay, New York, on May 22, 1919. She was 267 feet long, and her gross tonnage was 2564. Commissioned in December, she carried coal on the east coast for three months, then went aground in a February snow storm on the Cilley Ledge, off Port Clyde, Maine, where she lay for three years before sliding off the ledge to sink in deep water.

But the *Polias* was not the first seagoing American concrete cargo vessel.

William Leslie Comyn of San Francisco had studied the Fougners' successes. After a golfing conversation with engineer Alan MacDonald, he decided in 1917 that reinforced concrete was a promising material for west coast shipbuilding, since the alternatives were green wood and scarce, expensive steel transported from the east. As early as 1917 Comyn, an Englishman by birth, with twenty years' experience in shipping, asked the USSB for funds to build a concrete ship, designed by marine engineers Alan MacDonald and Victor Poss. He could not get government funds for this pioneering venture because the Shipping Board had still not made up its mind about concrete. Nonetheless, in September 1917, Comyn formed the San Francisco Shipbuilding Company and borrowed enough capital locally to establish a shipyard on the tide flats of Redwood City, on the east shore of the San Francisco

Comparative Sizes of Concrete Ships

Ship	Length	Tonnage
Namsenfjord	84'	200
Polias	267'	2564
Faith	320'	3400
Palo Alto	434'	6144

Peninsula. MacDonald was superintendent of construction, with a crew of 150, few of whom had any shipbuilding experience. On March 14, 1918, six weeks after the concrete was poured, Comyn and MacDonald launched the *Faith*, 320 feet long, and of 3400 gross tons. She cost $750,000, which was more than expected, and her lines showed more utility than beauty, but her price was less than that of a comparable steel ship, she had been built in 73 days, and she promptly proved to be seaworthy.

Rudolph J. Wig, the Emergency Fleet Corporation's concrete engineer, was among the hundreds of guests at the launching, and stayed in the west to observe her sea tests. The New York Times reported on March 16 that President Woodrow Wilson had expressed considerable interest in the *Faith*, and very shortly after her April performance tests in the bay and off the coast of San Francisco the Shipping Board, with Wilson's approval and encouragement, promised the San Francisco Shipbuilding Company contracts for three more, and larger, concrete ships.

The 320-foot *Faith* was not only the first American concrete ship completed, but at the time of her launching the largest in the world. She was commissioned on May 13, 1918, and nine days later departed on her maiden voyage to Vancouver, with a cargo of copper ore and salt. Later that year she also went to Hawaii, Chile,

Launching of the Faith, *March 14, 1918.*

and through the Panama Canal to New York, where in November 1918, having covered some 15,000 miles, she was inspected with interest by shippers and shipbuilders. She was sold the next year to the French American Steamship Lines for $450,000, made two trips to Europe and at least two more to South America before she was sold at auction for $160,000 in New Orleans in December 1921, stripped of her machinery, towed to Cuba, and sunk as a breakwater.

CHAPTER III

Fougner vs. Foley

The *Faith* was aptly named.

Her successful maiden voyage to Vancouver solidly confirmed the Fougners' arguments to the Shipping Board; in April 1918, after consultation with the nation's best concrete engineers, elaborate structural testing, and much deliberation, the Concrete Ship program was funded, and well on its way.

Rudolph J. Wig, Head of the new program, prepared a plan to build half a million tons of concrete ships. With approval of Congress and President Woodrow Wilson, the Emergency Fleet Corporation contracted with shipbuilders in Wilmington, North Carolina, Mobile, Alabama, San Diego and San Francisco, California, and Jacksonville, Florida to begin their construction. The initial designs were for ships of 3500 deadweight tons (the size of the *Faith*, and slightly larger than the Fougners' *Polias*), but in the spring of 1918, before any of the first four ships had been completed, the Shipping Board increased the standard design for future ships to 7500 tons, more than doubling the new ships' capacity.

Because the *Faith* had shown so successfully that the San Francisco Shipbuilding Company could build stone ships, it was not surprising that Comyn's company was one of the first chosen. Each of five shipbuilders received a contract to build eight ships, subject, of course, to Congressional appropriations. On June 5, 1918, A.P. Wright, acting for the Shipping Board, leased Government Island, in the San Antonio Estuary, from the cities of Oakland and Alameda, for the next twenty-five years, for Comyn's shipyard.

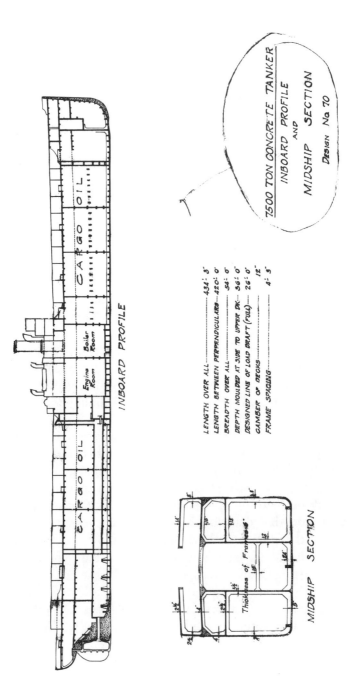

7500 TON CONCRETE TANKER
INBOARD PROFILE
AND
MIDSHIP SECTION
Design No. 70

INBOARD PROFILE

CARGO OIL

CARGO OIL

Boiler Room

Engine Room

LENGTH OVER ALL ———— 434'-3"
LENGTH BETWEEN PERPENDICULARS — 420'-0"
BREADTH OVER ALL ———— 54'-0"
DEPTH MOULDED AT SIDE TO UPPER DK.— 36½'-0"
DESIGNED LINE OF LOAD DRAFT (FULL)— 26'-0"
CAMBER OF DECKS ———— 12"
FRAME SPACING ———— 4'-3"

MIDSHIP SECTION

Thickness of Frames

Design plans for the enlarged size oil tankers, of which the Palo Alto was the first.

The San Francisco Shipbuilding Company promptly began construction of wooden forms and steel reinforcement for two tankers, to be called the *Palo Alto* and the *Peralta* (the *Peralta* was originally called the *Twilight*, which would have been appropriately prophetic, and less confusing than what was often spelled "Peralto" by the Washington bureaucracy).

Construction began with erection of outer wooden forms 40 feet high, 60 feet wide and almost 500 feet long. Inside each of these forms several miles of steel reinforcing rods were bent into position. Because of their weight, concrete hulls have to be relatively thin (the *Faith's* sides and bottom were 4.5 inches thick; the sides of the *Palo Alto* were four inches, the bottom five inches thick, braced by two foot beams at four foot intervals), Fougner's designs called for seven times as much steel as in land construction, 5% or more of the area of a cross section, whereas land structures required no more than 1%.

Building the forms for pouring the hull at the SF Shipbuilding Yard, Oakland, June 7, 1919.

When the steel skeleton was finished the inner forms were built, more intricate than the outer shells because they established varying thicknesses required for beams, engine mounts, and reinforcement of the rudder and propellor structures.

When the forms were complete, in late January 1919, the concrete mixture was prepared: the U.S. Shipping Board formula required one part Portland cement to two parts of aggregate (one third sand and two thirds gravel) to which water (15-20% of total volume) was added.

The cement for the *Palo Alto* and the *Peralta* came from Davenport, north of Santa Cruz. The San Francisco Shipbuilding Company specified light-weight slag, called puffed brick, for half the gravel, to reduce its weight. The concrete was mixed by machine for several minutes, poured into the forms and tamped to remove air pockets. Curing periods ranged from ten to twenty days.

Nicolay Fougner later expressed disapproval of puffed brick, assuming that the lighter aggregate weakened the concrete. He blamed it for the fate of the *Cape Fear*, one of the earlier USSB ships (267 feet long, with gross tonnage of 2795) finished before the Board settled on the 7500 ton standard. The hull of the *Cape Fear* was built with puffed-brick aggregate.

In late October 1920, while leaving Narragansett Bay, the *Cape Fear* collided with a steel ship loaded with granite, and sank in 3 minutes, taking 19 crew members with her. One survivor recalled that she "shattered like a teacup".

The teacup analogy was not lost on Paul Foley, a Navy captain assigned as the Emergency Fleet Corporation's Tank Steamer Executive in New York City. Foley's responsibility in 1919 was to dispose of USSB tankers at prices which would minimize the government's losses.

Captain Foley was a plain spoken man, never hesitant to express his opinion. Forthrightly he chastised the Board in early November 1919 when (in his words) they "released for industrial account eight concrete tank steamers [without consulting Tank Steamer Executive Foley] at a very attractive rate in a famine market, and ...chartered for an extended period the selected best tonnage so released to a single firm, without any announcement to the petroleum industry".

"Engine bed plate and crank shaft, S.S. Palo Alto. *July 7, 1919.*

"World's Largest Concrete Tanker". In drydock for cleaning, painting and repairs to hull. Moore Shipbuilding Co., Oakland.

WORLD'S LARGEST CONCRETE TANKER "PALO ALTO." 7,500 TONS D. W. CAPACITY, ON DRYDOCK FOR CLEANING, PAINTING AND REPAIRS TO HULL. MOORE SHIPBUILDING COMPANY, OAKLAND CAL. JUNE 18, 1920. 2198

Of the "selected best tonnage", Foley complained specifically about the leasing of four concrete tankers, the *Selma* and the *Latham*, both of 6278 tons, still under construction in Mobile, Alabama, the *Cuyamaca* (6486 tons) being built in San Diego, and the *Palo Alto* (6144 tons) being fitted in San Francisco, though not commissioned for another eleven months, in October 1920. The chairman of the Board, Judge J. B. Payne, who had sent Foley copies of the charter contracts which he had signed (leasing the ships to the American Fuel Oil and Transportation Company) was predictably embarrassed and annoyed.

Foley's objections, however, appear to have had some effect. The *Cuyamaca* charter was cancelled immediately, and the *Palo Alto's* soon thereafter. The *Selma* and the *Latham*, by then being operated by the Atlantic Refining Company, both ran aground on the Tampico jetty on the Mexican Gulf Coast (within a month of each other) and seriously damaged their hulls. The *Selma* was towed to Galveston for repairs and the *Latham*, temporarily patched, arrived there a day later under her own power. The *Latham* was

The concrete ship Atlantis, *also built to haul cargo during WW1, was brought to Cape May Point, New Jersey to serve as a ferry landing. A storm broke it from its mooring and the ferry project did not materialize. The sign on the side of the* Atlantis *is not a "keep off" sign, but advertises, "FOR BOAT INSURANCE. A.M. BIANCHI".*

sufficiently restored to return to Mobile in 1921. She was decommissioned at Mobile in 1926, and moved to New Orleans, where she was reported in the late twenties used as a floating storage tank. The *Selma* was dismantled and abandoned near Galveston in 1922.

Paul Foley had been promoted, and was the Shipping Board's Director of Operations when, in late October 1920 the Lincoln Steamship Line, of New York City, contracted with the U.S.S.B. to buy the *Palo Alto* for $780,000 and the *Peralta* for $765,000. The Board had offered them to the Lincoln Line on generous terms: 2.5% with the contract, 7.5% more at the time of delivery in San Francisco, and the balance in ten equal semi-annual installments, with 5% interest on the unpaid balance. The Board felt, however that oil prices and the capacities of the new ships would easily support these payments.

The *Palo Alto* was the first finished, and the Continental Trust Company, in the Lincoln Line's behalf, paid the $19,500 deposit to buy her. Robert Gomez, president of the Lincoln Line, found two interested New York businessmen, Martin Spielberg and George Williams, willing to invest in the *Palo Alto*. Spielberg and Williams arrived in Washington on Friday, November 26, carrying $59,000 in cash to make the second payment.

When they got to the Emergency Fleet Corporation offices they met the Board's chief telephone operator, E. H. Duff, and when he discovered the reason for their visit he suggested that they talk to Captain Foley. They asked Foley's opinion, as the Board's Chief of Operations, of the two ships in which they were about to invest.

Captain Foley told them promptly and unequivocally that neither of the concrete ships was "worth a God damn, that any contact with dock fenders would punch holes in them, and that any man who would risk a dollar on either of them would be a God damn fool!"

Spielberg and Williams, taken aback, pocketed their money and returned to New York, the Lincoln Line contract was cancelled (although the Board kept the $19,500 deposit), and the news of Captain Foley's candor spread along the waterfront.

A month after the *Palo Alto* was commissioned, prospects of her sale were fading. On January 3, 1921, the Board advertised the *Palo Alto*, the *Peralta*, and the *Latham* for charter leasing.

It was in preparation for charter service that the *Palo Alto* made the only voyages of record under her own power. On January 2, 1921, she sailed across San Francisco Bay, from the Bethlehem Shipbuilding Company, in Alameda, to the Hunter's Point drydock, arriving at 8 p.m. John Gaston, assigned as Chief Engineer, recorded this excursion in her log book, which was still aboard in 1930, though it has since disappeared. After three weeks in drydock the log recorded another voyage, on January 24, to busy Pier 33, on San Francisco's embarcadero, arriving at three o'clock in the afternoon, for display to potential charter customers.

In January the Board succeeded in leasing the *Latham*, which was in Galveston for repairs, but the only offers of record for the *Palo Alto* and *Peralta* (the latter finished in mid-January) came eleven months later from a man in San Francisco who wanted to sink them for a breakwater. Board Vice President Edward P. Farley declined this bid, saying that both ships were new, seaworthy, and at least suitable for oil storage. Farley suggested some of the Board's surplus wooden hulls as good breakwater material.

The S.S. Palo Alto crossing San Francisco Bay, January, 1921, all systems functioning.

Nevertheless, concrete tankers were not easily sold. As Sales Manager J. Harry Philbin observed, "Ship owners are suspicious of them and do not consider them to be practicable operating units, and it has been reported that both hull and cargo insurance is unobtainable for them."

The *Palo Alto's* log did not record whether she sailed or was towed, some weeks later, to the Benicia anchorage, boneyard of the Moth Ball Fleet.

In May Captain Foley resigned as the Emergency Fleet Corporation's Director of Operations; shortly thereafter he was assigned as aide to Navy Secretary Curtis Dwight Wilbur, but his Shipping Board days were not immediately forgotten.

In February 1922 the Continental Trust Company sought to recover its $19,500 deposit. Otis B. Kent, their attorney, described "Captain Foley's indiscretion" in some considerable detail; the Board's counsel recommended returning the money, and it was refunded.

The *Peralta* sold in July 1924 for a miserable $12,500, to the Portland Cement Company, which removed her engine and re-sold her the following year. She was fitted as a fish cannery, and was reported in 1941 to be moored in Richmond, California. She processed fish for over twenty years in San Francisco, Monterey, and San Diego Bays. John A. Campbell of Powell River, British Columbia, an authority on ferro-concrete ships, reports that the *Peralta* was towed to Powell River in 1959, to plug a gap in a floating mill-pond breakwater that had been in place since 1930.

The Peralta *as part of a breakwater at Powell River, British Columbia, 2001.*

Campbell stated in February 2002 that, after 82 years she was still afloat in the breakwater along with nine concrete hulls of WWII vintage, though almost having sunk on one occasion and currently undergoing negotiations to be intentionally sunk as an artificial reef.

In November 1924 Ship Sales Manager Harry Philbin reported that he had received a bid of $18,750 for the *Palo Alto*. Though she had cost $1.5 million only five years earlier, the way stone ships were going in the summer of 1924 Philbin decided that it was an acceptable price. It was, after all, fifty percent better than what they'd received for the *Peralta*. The buyer agreed to the Shipping Board's removal of the engine, within a year of the sale. The *Palo Alto* was towed off the muddy bottom at Benicia and prepared for transfer to her new owners.

The old pier, near Aptos Creek, about 1885. Originally built on Rafael Castro's land in the mid-1800's by Titus Hale, this pier was rebuilt and enlarged by 1880 by Claus Spreckels, who used it to ship lumber to Hawaii.

Not a drop of oil ever tainted these walls. Looking into the hold today.

CHAPTER IV

Final Voyage

During October and November 1924 there was a lively exchange of correspondence between J.J. Dwyer, USSB counsel in San Francisco and the prospective buyer, the Oliver J. Olson Company (also of San Francisco), over a $613.90 bill for towing the *Palo Alto* to deep water from the Benicia mud flats, which service, Olson reminded Dwyer, was not a part of the sales contract. Uncle Sam finally paid the bill, and the sale proceeded. It was registered on December 22, in the Solano County Courthouse in Fairfield, and a few days later in the U.S. Customs House in San Francisco.

Olson bought the ship as an oil storage barge, but the oil storage market didn't materialize. The *Palo Alto* was towed, some months later, to the Moore Shipbuilding Company, in Oakland. There her (almost new) 2800 h.p. Llewellyn reciprocating engine, two hundred foot steel shaft (18 inches in diameter) and fifteen foot bronze propeller were removed for the Shipping Board, and the five year old tanker was laid up, once more for sale. Lynn Lindquist, recalling these events in a 1972 article in *National Fisherman*, could account for neither engine nor shaft, but reported that the propeller was shipped to Hamburg in 1929.

The *Palo Alto* spent another five idle years tied up in San Francisco Bay. In 1929 she belonged to an Oakland machinery dealer named R. C. Porter. In the fall of that year he succeeded in selling her to the Seacliff Amusement Corporation (chartered in Nevada) for an undisclosed amount of cash, some stock in the company, and a seat on the Board of Directors.

The Seacliff Amusement Corporation was formed in 1929, and lasted less than three years, only the first of which could be

"Map of Seacliff Park District. Showing Subdivided and Unsubdivided lands and Development Units, Santa Cruz County, California. June 1926." Though never built, the street layout is similar to what was eventually done.

Detail from map: in addition to a natatorium and concessions,they thought they might capture a little of the ocean as well. Note the airplane frolicking.

described as prosperous. The urge to build a resort on Seacliff Beach was a twentieth century, west coast splinter of Manifest Destiny, but this was the beginning of the great depression.

The beautiful arc of coast from the Rio Del Mar to China Beach (now New Brighton), east of Capitola, had inspired the Seacliff Company of Santa Cruz to prepare, in 1925 and 1926, an ambitious development plan for Seacliff Beach and the coastal plateau above it, with a clubhouse, a large auditorium, a breakwater, a hotel, and a residential subdivision which reached from the bluffs back to the Watsonville-Santa Cruz Road.

The Seacliff Beach resort projected the hospitable tradition of Claus Spreckels, whose mansion, guest houses, hotel, deer park, stables, race track, and polo grounds transformed the wooded hills and beach which he bought from the Aptos Rancho estate of Don Rafael Castro. It was a particularly beautiful beach, only a few hours' drive from San Francisco and the Santa Clara Valley, unoccupied in 1925 except for the tar paper shack of an eccentric named Paul Woodside. Woodside died in September of that year in a shootout which also killed Sheriff Howard Trafton and Deputy

"The madman of the cliffs", Paul Woodside, in a calmer moment at his cabin above the beach at Seacliff. Note the many structures on the beach below, circa 1925.

Dick Rountree, who had come to serve commitment papers.

The Seacliff Company's major initial investment was in a seawall along the beach, the cost of which preempted most of the available capital. The new seawall was destroyed by winter surf a few months after it was built, and the developers never recovered from this loss. Nevertheless, the beauty of the beach and the urge to develop it survived.

The Seacliff Amusement Corporation was formed to develop what the *Santa Cruz Sentinel* later described as "a most unique amusement enterprise", a 430 foot ship moored on the Seacliff beach, aboard which would be dining, dancing, swimming, fishing, and whatever other forms of entertainment the public required and the law would allow.

The first president of the corporation was a retired Salt Lake City druggist named F.J. Banks; Alfred L. Tamblin, an insurance agent and mayor of Ely, Nevada and H. O. Heiner of Santa Cruz were vice presidents; other board members were George Humes and Charles M. Erb of Seacliff, Charles Sing and Stanley C. Evans of Ely, former owner R. C. Porter, and Harold Tribe, a real estate agent from Ogden, Utah. All the officers of the Corporation had survived the stock market crash the previous October with enough capital to invest

Coast and land inland of Seacliff Beach when the Palo Alto *arrived, 1931. This is the land the Seacliff Company wanted to develop.*

in an almost-sure thing at Seacliff Beach on Monterey Bay.

At four o'clock in the afternoon of Tuesday, January 21, 1930 the *Palo Alto* began her final voyage, from the Moore Shipbuilding Yard in Oakland to Seacliff Beach on Monterey Bay, towed by a Red Stack tug, under orders to keep her speed under five knots. Among her passengers were former owner R. C. Porter, Treasurer Charles Erb, and Warren Loughery of Soquel. She was top-heavy without an engine, and one of the passengers was apprehensive at the way she rolled when she reached the open sea. Nevertheless she arrived safely at Seacliff at 7 a.m. on Wednesday, January 22, 1930.

Tom Lindsey of Capitola was engaged to mark with buoys the places for anchors. The beginnings of a pier were already under construction, somewhat west of where Claus Spreckels's pier had stood beside Aptos Creek at the turn of the century. The *Palo Alto* had to be anchored in line with the pier. The tug stayed for two days, during which the ship's three 3.5 ton anchors were lowered. A steel cable was drawn from the stern through a block on one of the pier pilings, and a gasoline-powered winch on the after deck pulled the *Palo Alto* in toward the beach.

On Saturday the 25th, her owners satisfied with her position,

Red Stack tug positions S.S. Palo Alto at Seacliff Beach on the morning of January 22, 1930.

*Note the
unfinished pier
with derrick.*

A couple of observers watch the positioning. Note the lack of vegetation on the cliff.

S.S. Palo Alto, *home at last; 1930.*

the crew opened the seacocks in the boiler room, and she settled
to the bottom. That day's news accounts announced plans for a
restaurant on the top deck, "100 staterooms, and several well-
furnished and comfortable salons."

In the spring of 1930, as work advanced on the ship and the
pier, the Seacliff Amusement Corporation borrowed $28,000 from
the Calavada Investment Company (not Cal-Neva or Cal-Nevada,
as the Seacliff Amusement Company has often been called) of
Ely, Nevada to finish and equip her, finish the pier, dig a 190 foot
well for fresh water, and pave the access road down from the
Watsonville-Santa Cruz Road and along the beach. The Calavada
Investment Company, of which James Lockhart was President,
derived much of its capital from the big copper mine near Ely.

Building the last five yards of the pier proved difficult: a ledge
of rock frustrated the pile driver, and well-drilling equipment was
required to sink nine-foot holes to receive the pilings. Bert Duer, a
well driller, sank the holes, eighteen inches in diameter, and
inserted steel drill casings to keep the sand out. The projected
opening date of June 1 was put off; while the drilling proceeded the
construction crew rode a tram out to the ship to complete the

Workmen on the tram going out to the ship from the unfinished pier.

The road down to the beach at Seacliff before it was paved.

building of the superstructure and finish the interior.

The infusion of new capital from Nevada brought with it some new faces on the Board. Dr. R. A. Bowdle, chief surgeon of the Nevada Consolidated Copper Company's big mine at McGill, near Ely, replaced F. J. Banks as president, George C. Humes of Aptos, who provided, among other necessities, the three inch redwood planks for the pier, was vice president, and Charles M. Erb, also of Aptos, became secretary-treasurer. Other members of the Board at the Ship's debut were J.C. Kinnear, the copper mine's general manager, Ely banker O.G. Bates, J. H. Eager, Ely's Ford dealer, F. E. Huffer of McGill, a copper mine official, C. A. Stone, theatre owner in Ely, and Stanley Draper, of McGill.

The Board visited Seacliff during the last week of May, to announce that The Ship would open on June 14, and that "every effort will be made to retain the nautical atmosphere of the huge seven story boat". They also approved manager Raymond Carpenter's award of the restaurant concession to Tom Roussel and Frank Wagner, both of San Francisco, and the dance hall management to Stanley Evans of Ely, one of the original board members.

CHAPTER V

Halcyon Days of *the Ship*

The *Palo Alto*, her big white superstructure gleaming at the end of the pier (630 feet long and 40 feet wide, finished in early June) opened the Rainbow Ballroom on Saturday, June 21, 1930, for a special preview. The dance hall occupied most of the main deck, and was 54 feet wide, with tall windows looking out over the Bay. Several hundred people spent the inaugural evening dancing to the music of Ed Rookledge's ten piece orchestra, or playing Bingo in the amusement arcade.

Parking on the pier, for your convenience.

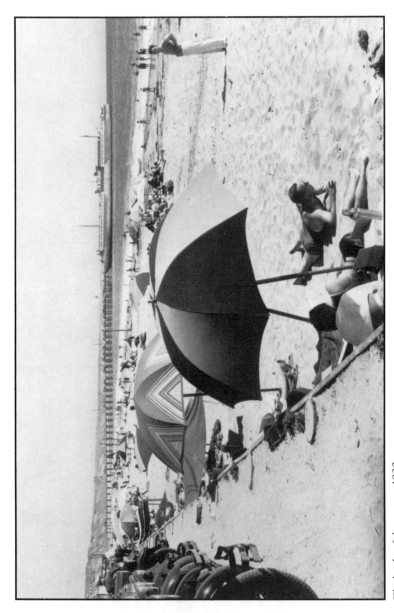

The height of the season, 1930.

Ad from the Register-Pajaronian for opening night, 1930. Note the smokestack drawn in, to prove that it's a ship.

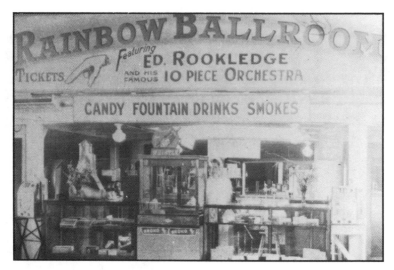

Concession stand at the Rainbow Ballroom.

"Famous dance orchestra in 'Rainbow' Ballroom". The Rookledge Orchestra ready to play.

"Dancing in the Rainbow Ballroom".

"Dining saloon". At one point known as the "Fish Palace".

The official opening, suitably advertised, was the following Saturday night, when there was also a major convention in Santa Cruz of the Veterans of Foreign Wars. If they drove down the Watsonville-Santa Cruz Road the neon THE SHIP sign at the Seacliff turnoff guided them down to the beach.

The Ship itself was ablaze with lights, white ash decks and brass fittings gleaming, pennants flying from her 76 foot masts, the pier and beachfront drive crowded with cars. The Rainbow Ballroom was again filled with the music of Ed Rookledge, the Ship Cafe and Fish Restaurant (forward, on the bridge deck) served dinner, and the swimming pool (in the former engine room) the fishing deck on the bow, and 23,000 feet of promenade deck were open for inspection.

The *Santa Cruz Sentinel*'s headline was "MOST UNIQUE AMUSEMENT ENTERPRISE MAKES ITS BOW". There were bingo, slot machines, and other carnival entertainments such as the Ham and Bacon Game, the Airplane Race, and Pitch Till You Win. The arcade was full of the fragrance of hot dogs, and although it was not a conspicuous amenity, old timers recall that one might with suitable discretion obtain a bottle of bootleg booze.

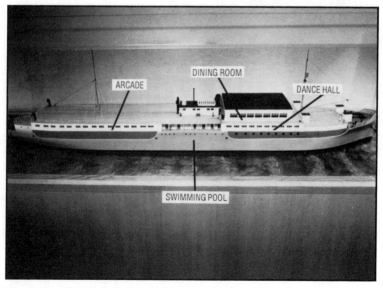

The model of the S.S. Palo Alto built by Tom Fordham and on display in the visitor center, with locations of the entertainment areas.

The ferry *Markel* made two round trips every evening from the Santa Cruz wharf, with a stop each way at Capitola. The fare was a dollar round trip. That evening, the Ship Cafe invited 150 local people to a special banquet. The *Sentinel* reported that two thousand cars visited Seacliff Beach that weekend, and that three thousand people boarded the *Palo Alto*.

The Ship was launched.

Marvin Ennis, a retired Navy warrant officer who graduated in the early thirties from Watsonville high school, recalls with pleasure attending a Spring Formal in the Rainbow Ballroom, and dining in the Ship Cafe, where he found the food to be very good. It was a festive occasion, enhanced, he remembers, by a hip-flask of liquor which one of his classmates filled occasionally from a bottle hidden somewhere outside.

Charles G. Erb, son of Charles M. Erb who was secretary – treasurer of the Seacliff Amusement Corporation, has recently provided his recollections of the events of 1930 and immediately thereafter, admittedly influenced by his parent's stories as he was five years old at the time. He recalls that local artichoke farmer and house-builder named Bert Wible brought Charles Sr. into the plan, but that Wible pulled out and moved to San Jose when gambling and liquor money from Ely and Las Vegas, Nevada became part of the deal. The younger Charles Erb remembers that games of chance were in the former engine room, and doubts whether a swimming pool could have been in there. His parents repeatedly told stories of the landing of liquor there while the Coast Guard stood off, and that the cases of booze were stored in the surrounding orchards above the beach to conceal them. Interestingly, he also heard stories for which no records have been found of one of the managers being killed in a power-play in Nevada, and a subsequent shoot-out on the beach at which a local was injured.

In 1978 in the *Sentinel*, Wallace Wood published a purported reminiscence of a conversation with Gladys Erb, whose husband Tilman Erb was a stockholder, and who remembered The Ship fondly. Her stories, as Wood recorded them, were exciting, colorful, and full of nostalgia. She recalled that the company paid $300,000 for the *Palo Alto*, (unlikely, since Olsen had paid only eighteen thousand six years earlier), that a disgruntled stockholder had

*The young Charles
Erb, Stevie Duer,
and Ed Gillette.*

threatened to dynamite the hull, and that the corporation was
called the Cal-Neva Amusement Center, a name of which there is
no contemporary record. Wood also listed the major dance bands,
including Paul Whiteman's, Benny Goodman's and Tommy
Dorsey's, which Mrs. Erb recalled hearing in the Rainbow Ballroom,
making no mention of Ed Rookledge, of Jean Drury and the Three
Rhythm Girls, of Tony Landrum's banjo, or of George Cracknell's
Greater Marine Ballroom Orchestra, whose performances earlier
Sentinels recorded. Although Mrs. Erb's reminiscence (as recalled
by Wood) must have been somewhat embroidered, it was evocative
of the halcyon summer of 1930.

The Ship's business fell off during the winter of 1930-31, most
of which it was closed.

Late in May 1931, H.E. Gillette, a new manager, announced
the Grand Reopening of the Rainbow Ballroom on Memorial Day,
with dancing beginning at 10 A.M. to the music of Jean Drury
and the Three Rhythm Girls, and the reopening of the redecorated
Cafe, serving "regular lunch and dinner at popular prices (Sixty
cents for lunch, Eighty-five for dinner), ample parking space, and
free picnic space". The preceding day the Santa Cruz Superior
Court heard a suit brought by the Seacliff Amusement Corporation
against Arthur and Ruth Levin, the bingo concessionaires,
presumably for delinquent payment.

In July the Rainbow Ballroom was open on Saturday nights,
featuring the Greater Marine Ballroom Orchestra, conducted by
George Cracknell of Salinas, with Tony Landrum of Santa Cruz
on the banjo.

On August 8, 1931 the State of California acquired the first
parcel of Seacliff Beach from the Santa Cruz Land Title Company.

The winter of 1932 was a stormy one; the road down to the beach washed out, and the pounding surf produced a crack in the hull amidships, forward of the swimming pool.

That crack in the hull was the beginning of the end of The Ship, and of the Seacliff Amusement Corporation. The road to the beach was repaired in the spring, but The Ship was boarded up. On April 26, 1932 the Calavada Investment Company filed a notice of default against the Seacliff Amusement Corporation, and engaged the Santa Cruz Land Title Company as trustee to retrieve whatever was left of their investment. The Santa Cruz Land Title Company as trustee for the Calavada Investment Company sold itself the land for a bargain price of $10,000, sold The Ship back to the Calavada Investment Company for ten dollars, and offered the beach to the State of California as part of a gift-sale transaction which established Seacliff Beach State Park.

In this transaction the state of California acquired 3150 feet of beach land for Seacliff Beach State Park, part by purchase, part by gift, from Beldon Bias and H.O.Heiner of the Santa Cruz Land Title Company. Simultaneously and in the same transaction the state acquired 6600 feet of beachfront at Sunset Beach. The appraised value reported for both was $230,000, the purchase price $115,000.

The Aptos Beach Inn later filled the entertainment niche that the Palo Alto carved out. Built 1932.

One of the Seacliff Company's aspirations, a resort hotel, was realized in 1932 just east of Aptos Creek at Rio Del Mar. There the Aptos Beach Inn, built the year the Seacliff Amusement Company collapsed, grew and flourished for a decade, was enlarged in 1937, closed during the Second World War, reopened in 1957 and was destroyed by fire in 1963. In her *Santa Cruz County, Parade of the Past*, Margaret Koch recalls the halcyon days of the late thirties at the Aptos Beach Inn, which featured such famous band leaders as Ted Fio Rito, Carl Ravazza, and Hal Pruden: "Those were the days when an evening of dinner dancing — a 'big evening'— cost maybe $5 or $10". She also recalls that when the hotel burned, on March 17, 1963 "some 300 guests celebrating St. Patrick's Day there were herded out to safety as the flames crackled through the structure."

All that remains of the *S.S.Palo Alto*, still settled into the sand at Seacliff Beach, is a monument to the importance of timing.

She was the first 7500-ton concrete tanker to be launched on the Pacific Coast, but by the time she was ready to put to sea in October 1920, the wartime market for tankers (particularly "crockery tankers", as their critics called them) had evaporated. The nudge from Captain Foley was all she needed to consign her to the Benicia mud flats.

The Seacliff Amusement Corporation, which rescued her from Benicia ten years later and transformed her into a bright seaside pleasure dome, filed its articles of incorporation in Nevada less than three months after the stock market crash of October 29, 1929.

Although the Depression was only beginning, it was an inauspicious time: a year later President Hoover asked Congress for $150 million in Employment Relief, because there were over a quarter million Americans out of work. By August 1932, when it sold its beach land, the Calavada Investment Company had lost most of its stake in The Ship.

The *Palo Alto's* white superstructure was boarded up that year, and her stone hull broke amidships, for the first time, under the slow relentless pounding of the sea.

CHAPTER VI

The Fishing Era

In l934, after she had lain abandoned for two years, a weathered relic of the great depression, a wrecker named H. R. Lord bought from the Calavada Investment Company the right to dismantle the *Palo Alto*'s superstructure and to sell everything salvagable. Furniture, kitchen equipment, bronze and brass fittings, and finally the lumber in the decks and outer wooden walls, went to the highest bidder, at depression prices. In the three years since the summer of l930 the proud and festive Ship had changed its face and its function. Dancing, dining, and games of chance were replaced as entertainments aboard the cement ship by fishing and quiet contemplation of the endless motion of the sea.

On February 12, l936 the California Division of Parks bought the *Palo Alto* for one dollar from Arthur H. Wikkerink and Walter F. Pilgrim, who had acquired it from the Calavada Investment Company. On December 22, 1948 the tidelands and bottom around the ship (eighty feet wide and extending beyond the bow) were formally and officially transferred to the Park Service by the State Lands Commission.

Seacliff State Beach had a fishing pier.

In l939 severe winter storms enlarged the crack in the hull, but she held her own for almost twenty more years. In l958 the foredeck was closed as unsafe. In l959 the Hiley Tree Service of Felton felled her 76-foot masts, which Park Supervisor Evon Till judged to be sufficiently rotten as to be hazardous.

During the nineteeen fifties Ralph Creffield's bait and tackle shop occupied the stern cabin, where he also rented rowboats with

By 1948, the crack is just starting to separate the bow from the stern.

1951.

By 1958, the crack is showing real separation.

Creffield's Bait Stand in stern cabin, late '40's or early '50's.

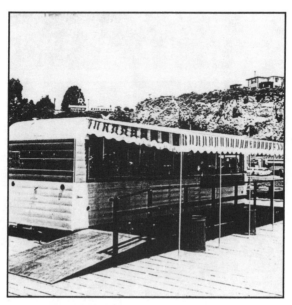

First Creffield Hamburger Stand, installed about 1945.

Moving the hamburger stand off the pier in 1983. It now stands next to the road near the entry to the pier.

This 1950 newspaper pictorial feature shows fun on the boat.

From a perch on the anchor winch Betty's twin sister, Beverly, points out familiar landmarks to Bob Johnson.

outboard motors (Creffield built the boats and maintained them himself), which he stored on deck and lowered over the port side with a small crane. Passengers descended a thirty foot stairway to the launching dock below. Creffield also had a hamburger stand, in a trailer installed about 1945, at the entrance to the pier. A larger, wooden hamburger stand was built there in the early sixties, and moved in 1983 to the beach across the road from the pier, where it survives today.

Fishing from the old ship has always been good. As one fisherman wrote in 1961, it combined "the advantages of deep sea and surf fishing. You can still get almost a thousand feet offshore," he said, "far enough to go after the big ones that don't venture too close to the surf."

In 1962 Ralph Stanton, owner of the Valley Sport Shop in Watsonville, proposed sinking another concrete ship alongside the *Palo Alto*. By 1962, however concrete ships were in short supply, so the scheme came to naught.

In early 1963 winter storms broke the hull where it had cracked in 1932, and the bow settled several feet into the sand. More heavy weather in January 1978 increased the break in the hull amidships,

1991. The two halves of the ship continue to separate.

1991 view of damaged below-decks. Probably "tank #3 center".

causing all but the stern to settle to starboard. Heavy seas tore pilings loose from the pier; they battered and weakened those still standing. Enough of the pier's planks were gone that it was closed as unsafe.

The *Palo Alto* and the pier were closed for most of the next five years, and the park administration, under heavy pressure to commit their funds to rebuilding Seacliff's popular trailer camp on the beach — washed away in 1978 — could not afford to restore them. There were more destructive storms in January 1980, and the park regretfully announced that the Cement Ship would be closed indefinitely. In March 1978 Jack Costello, the maintenance supervisor of the park, said "I question if it will ever be opened again." Presently three local fishermen, distressed by this announcement, were scheming to rescue the ship and the pier.

Rose Costa is a short, dynamic woman who lives just above Seacliff Beach. She takes her fishing seriously, and recalls with some pride the season when she caught 52 salmon, most of them from the deck of the *Palo Alto*.

Storm of '80 washes over both sides of the hull

Storm of February 1983 batters the Palo Alto.

Driftwood, sometimes full trees washed out of the Santa Cruz mountains, down the creeks and to the Bay, come to rest on shore after battering the Palo Alto and breakwaters.

Wobbly pier and eroded beach after the '83 storms

Rebar madness, as the concrete wears away and the rebar contorts.

Rose Costa and Harry Haney, leaders of the "Save our Ship" movement, take a break during the '83 repairs.

With fellow fishermen Harry Haney and Ed Nelson she concluded that it was time to save the old ship, and that it was up to them to do it. Early in 1983 Costa remembers that she, Haney, and Nelson telephoned everyone they knew who might be able to help. Park Superintendant Dick Menafee was able to find funds for new deck planks on the pier; the Granite Rock Company and the Jimmie Smith Plumbing Company of Soquel helped with materials, and they found that a lot of people were willing to work to save the old cement ship.

From February until July, Boy Scout Troop 616, fraternity men from San Jose State, soldiers from Fort Ord, neighbors, fishermen, and members of the Monterey Bay Natural History Association spent long, strenuous weekends replacing 68 big deck planks on the pier, carrying sixteen tons of asphalt in wheelbarrows to refinish the deck of the ship, and rebuilding iron safety rails.

Rose Costa was everywhere, with tools, nails, appreciation, and encouragement. She estimated afterward that the volunteers had given 8,000 hours of work, which saved the State at least $50,000. On July 23, 1983 The *Palo Alto* was reopened, in a ceremony attended by Senator Henry Mello, Assemblyman Sam Farr, Supervisor Robley Levy, and State Park Rangers Menafee, Larry Cermak,

"Palo Alto clean-up day, April 23, 1983. Sponsored by the Monterey Bay Natural History Association".

Replacing pier planks after '80 storm.

People crowd the sides. Frequent mackerel runs brought capacity crowds. This photo shows a day before 1959, when the masts were cut.

and Jim Fife, and 350 volunteers, *Palo Alto* enthusiasts, and fishermen, ready to resume their posts along the newly restored railing.

The old ship was once more in good condition — up to the chain link fence amidships, through which the wreckage of the broken forecastle loomed in the distance, covered with pelicans and white with their droppings. Once more the deck was crowded with fishermen, particularly in July 1984, when there was a spectacular run of mackerel.

But the pier was not what it had been before the storms of 1978, and the following year it was closed again while 37 pilings were replaced. After reopening briefly it was closed again for a good part of 1986, while a Morro Bay Contractor replaced eighteen more pilings and several dozen deck planks. The ship was closed again on October 27th, 2001 because of progressive storm damage.

The *Palo Alto* has subsided perceptibly under the pounding of the sea during her three score years at Seacliff, but she is a tough old stone ship, and Rose Costa and her fishing friends expected her to give the same pleasure to a few more generations of fishermen and marine birdwatchers that she has given to them.

Major pier repairs in 1985.

Whether she lasts another sixty years depends on the moods of the Pacific Ocean. In January 1978, after that winter's destructive storm, State Parks Area Manager Harold Bradshaw requested funds for an engineering inspection of the old hull, and talked seriously about demolishing it, which he figured to cost two to three million dollars.

Chief Ranger Bob Culbertson, who has seen the Seacliff sea wall destroyed three times, acknowledges the uncertain future of the *Palo Alto* and the pier.

"I know what the ocean can do when it's really angry out there", says Culbertson, "The pier might last another sixty, even two hundred years, but others (at Rio del Mar, at Sunset Beach, and at Moss Landing, for example) have disappeared, pounded by floating logs and big breakers."

The State Parks Division will keep the old ship open for fishermen as long as she is safe. Even when the seas have pounded her down there is no thought of removing her. The old hull is already a fine fish habitat, and more breaks below the waterline can only make her more hospitable to the bass, perch, salmon and rockfish who find shelter in her broken hold.

When the deck is no longer safe for fishing the Division's plan is to extend the pier out around her. Whatever is left of the shell of the old ship will be left as a home for the fish. People looking down from the pier will see the fish in their habitat, but also some of the chine of the bow, the sturdy reinforcing beams, a porthole amidships, the stern hawser sheaves, and other reminders of the tanker *Palo Alto*, and of the winter day in 1921 when she steamed proudly up the Bay from Hunter's Point to Pier 33 on the Embarcadero, oblivious to the unpleasant fact that she was government surplus.

Forever facing south, but with friends.

Appendix 1
Timeline

Dates Important to the S.S. Palo Alto

Date	National Event	YEAR	Date	S.S. *Palo Alto* Event
Apr 6	US declares war on Germany	**1917**		
Aug 2	Fougner launches *Namsenfjord*			
March	Comyn launches *Faith*	**1918**	Apr 12	Wilson appropriates $ for concrete ships
Nov 11	Armistice Day: WW1 ends		June 5	Government Island leased for Comyn
		1919	Jan 20	First ship concrete poured
May 22	Fougner launches *Polias*		May 29	*Palo Alto* launched near Oakland
October	*Cape Fear* sinks in 3 minutes	**1920**	October	P.A. commissioned
			Nov 26	Foley gives bad opinion to buyers
		1921	Jan 21	P.A. sails across SF Bay on only powered trip
		1924	Dec 22	Sold for scrap
Oct 29	Stock market crash	**1929**		Propellor shipped to Hamburg, Germany
		1930	January	Seacliff Amusement Corp files to incorporate
			Jan 21	P.A. towed from Oakland
			Jan 22	Arrives Aptos
			Jan 25	Settles to bottom
			June 21	Preview opening of Rainbow Ballroom
			June 28	Official opening
August	State of California starts to acquire Seacliff Beach	**1931**		

Date	National Event	YEAR	Date	S.S.*Palo Alto* Event
		1932	winter	Storms crack hull Seacliff Amusement Corp. collapses
		1934		H.R. Lord buys *P.A.* for scrap
		1936	Feb 12	*P.A.* bought by California Division of Parks
		1939	winter	Storms enlarge crack
	WW2 ends	1945		Creffield builds hamburger stand on pier
		1948	Dec 22	Tidelands near ship officially transferred to Park Service
		1958		Foredeck closed as unsafe
		1959		Masts toppled and cut up
Nov	President Kennedy assassinated	1963		Storms break hull where crack was
		1978	January	Storms increase break amidships; closed
		1983	July 23	Reopened
		1984		Closed while pilings replaced
		1986		Closed while pilings, deck planks replaced

APPENDIX 2

Descending Value of Ship

Date	Place	Owner	Purpose	Amount Paid
May 29, 1919	Alameda/Oakland	U.S. Shipping Board	Safe oil shipping	$1,500,000
(Oct. 20, 1920	SF then Benecia	Lincoln Steamship Line	Safe oil shipping)	$780,000
Dec. 22, 1924	Oakland	Oliver J. Olson Co.	Oil Storage barge	$18,750
Late 1929	Oakland	R.C. Porter	Machinery	?
Jan. 21, 1930	To Seacliff Beach	Calavada Investment Co.	"Amusement Enterprise"	?
April 26, 1932	Seacliff Beach	Calavada II	Liquidation of Assets	$10
1936	Seacliff Beach	Arthur H. Wikkerink & Walter F. Pilgrim	Fishing Pier	?
Feb. 2, 1936	Seacliff Beach	California Div. of Parks	Fishing Pier	$1
?2000?	Seacliff Beach	California Div. of Parks	Estimated cost to scrap & clean up	$2,500,000

Notes

Correspondence, unless otherwise cited, is from the National Archives, Record Group 32 (United States Shipping Board Emergency Fleet Corporation).

Chapter I

San Francisco Chronicle, May 30, 1919, p.3.

San Francisco Examiner, May 30, 1919, p.21.

Letter, Rudolph Wig to Patrick Hurley, May 29, 1919.

United States Shipping Board Emergency Fleet Corporation. *Second Annual Report, 1918*, p.2-6.

——————— *Fifth Annual Report, 1921*, p.247

——————— *Emergency Fleet Corporation Personnel*, 1919, p.3.

Lindquist, Lynn. "Concrete Tanker Project Recorded in Photos", *National Fisherman*, v. 53, pp.10B-11B, May, 1972.

Letter, Chauncey Parker to J. J. Dwyer, January 2, 1925.

Santa Cruz Sentinel, January 23, 1930, p.1, January 24, 1930, p.1 and January 25, 1930, p.1.

Letter, O. B. Kent to H. S. Kimball, February 2, 1922.

Chapter II

Fougner, Nicolay Knutzon. *Seagoing and Other Concrete Ships,* London, Frowde, Hodder, and Stoughton, 1922, ch. 1-3.

New York Times, June 11, 1918, p.5, July 28, 1918, p.3, and April 21, 1918.

"Present Status of the Concrete Ship" (summary of a report by H.C. Turner to the American Concrete Institute), *Scientific American Monthly,* v. 1, pp.380-381, April 1920.

Havilland, Jean. "American Concrete Steamers of the First and Second World Wars," *American Neptune,* v. 22, pp.157-183, July 1962.

McNairn, Jackson C. "America's Forgotten 'Crockery' Fleet", *U.S. Naval Institute Proceedings,* v. 67, no. 12, p.1740-42, December 1941.

"Use of Reinforced Concrete in Shipbuilding", *Science,* v. 49, p.419-20, May 2, 1919.

Letter, Paul Foley to J. B. Payne, November 6, 1919.

Chapter III

Emergency Fleet News, v. 1, no. 40, December 5, 1918, p.3.

New York Times, March 16, 1918, p.1, April 4, 1918, p.8, May 6, 1918, p.13, May 16, 1918, p.5, June 6, 1918, p.7, and June 11, 1918, p.5.

Havilland, *op. cit,* p.161 ff.

"Ships of Puffed Brick", *Scientific American*, v. 120, p.314, March 29, 1919.

San Francisco Chronicle, January 17, 1917, p.19 and May 1, 1918, p.17.

San Francisco Examiner, March 15, 1918, p.1.

Santa Cruz Sentinel, January 22, 1930, p.3 and February 2, 1930, p.3.

Letter, Paul Foley to J. B. Payne, November 6, 1919.

Memorandum from W. W. Nottingham to George E. Heerbrandt, December 3, 1919.

McNairn, *op. cit.*, p.1742.

Letter from Otis Really Kent to Harry S. Kimball, February 6, 1922.

Letter from J. Harry Philbin to L. C. Palmer, November 21, 1924.

Chapter IV

Memorandum from J. Harry Philbin to Chauncey G. Parker, November 28, 1924.

Letter, Chauncey G. Parker to J. J. Dwyer, December 10, 1924.

Telegram from J. J. Dwyer to Chauncey G. Parker, December 16, 1924.

Koch, Margaret. *Santa Cruz County; Parade of the Past*. Fresno, Valley Publishers, 1973, p.97-8.

Rowland, Leon. *Santa Cruz; The Early Years; The Collected Historical Writings of Leon Rowland*. Santa Cruz, Paper Vision Press, 1980, p.166.

Lindquist, *op. cit.*, p.10B.

Santa Cruz Sentinel, January 24, 1930, p.1, January 25, 1930, p.1, January 28, 1930, p.4, and January 29, 1930, p.3.

Chapter V

Santa Cruz Sentinel, May 29, 1931, p.3, June 20, 1930, p.7, June 21, 1930, p.1, June 25, 1930, p.1, June 28, 1930, p.4, June 29, 1930, p.3 and July 11, 1931, p.5.

Santa Cruz Evening News, June 28, 1930, p.2 and August 31, 1931, p.3.

Koch, Margaret, *op.cit.*, p.160.

Seacliff State Beach. *Unit History* (MS) 1931-1936 and grant deeds in the Santa Cruz County Recorder's Office.

Chapter VI

Seacliff State Beach. *Unit History* (MS) 1931-1986.

San Jose Mercury, January 26, 1978 p.10.

Santa Cruz Evening News, April 27, 1936, p.6.

Santa Cruz Sentinel, January 13, 1978, p.5.

Wanderer, Bob. "The Cement Ship", *National Motorist*, March-April 1961, pp.15-16.

Watsonville Register-Pajaronian, January 13, 1978, p.1; February 7, 1983, p.1; January 9, 1985, p.17; November 19, 1986, p.1.

Bibliography

California Department of Parks and Recreation. *Seacliff State Beach General Development Plan*, 1970. 35 p., 1 map.

Clark, Donald T. *Santa Cruz County Place Names*. Santa Cruz, Santa Cruz County Historical Society, 1986. 552 p.

Construction of Concrete Ships; Letters and Reports... U. S. 65th Congress, 2d Session. Senate Commerce Committee Report, (Senate Document 239). Washington, 1918. 58 p.

Erb, Charles G. *The Concrete Casino*. Virginia Beach, unpublished story, 2001. 19 p.

Fougner, Nicolay Knutzon. *Seagoing and Other Concrete Ships*. London, Frowde, Hodder, and Stoughton, 1922. 216 p.

Hart, James D. *A Companion to California*, New York, Oxford University Press, 1978. 504 p.

Havilland, Jean. "American Concrete Steamers of the First and Second World Wars," *American Neptune*, v. 22, p.157-183, July 1962.

Koch, Margaret. *Santa Cruz County; Parade of the Past*. Fresno, Valley Publishers, 1973. 254 p.

Lindquist, Lynn (Lindy). "Concrete Tanker Project Recorded in Photos," *National Fisherman*, v. 53, p.10A-B, May 1972.

Lloyd's Register of Shipping. *Register Book, 1921*. London, 1921.

McNairn, Jackson C. "America's Forgotten 'Crockery' Fleet," *U.S. Naval Institute Proceedings*, v. 67, no. 12, p. 1740-42, December 1941.

Morgan, Terri. "Ship Shape at Seacliff", *The Sun*, Santa Cruz, November 6, 1987.

The Moore Drydock Company. San Francisco, Schwabacher-Frey Company, [1946] 24 p.

The New York Times.

The Oakland Tribune.

Portland Cement Association. *Concrete Ships, a Possible Solution to the Shipping Problem*. Chicago, 1917. 46 p.

"Present Status of the Concrete Ship" (summary of a report by H.C. Turner to the American Concrete Institute), *Scientific American Monthly*, v. 1, PP.380-381, April 1920.

Rowland, Leon. *Santa Cruz; The early Years; The Collected Historical Writings of Leon Rowland*. Santa Cruz, Paper Vision Press, 1980.

The San Francisco Chronicle.

The San Francisco Examiner.

The San Jose Mercury.

The Santa Cruz City and County Directory, 1929-36.

The Santa Cruz Evening News.

The Santa Cruz Sentinel.

"Ships of Puffed Brick", *Scientific American*, v. 120, p. 314, March 29, 1919.

United State Board of Engineers for Rivers and Harbors. *The Ports of San Francisco, Oakland, Berkeley, Richmond...* Washington, 1933. 334 p.

United States Congress. Select Committee on U.S. Shipping Board Operations. *Shipping Board Operations*. Washington, 1920-21. 151 p.

United States Shipping Board Emergency Fleet Corporation. *Report*, 1918-22.

"Use of Reinforced Concrete in Shipbuilding", *Science*, v. 49, p. 419-29, May 2, 1919.

Wanderer, Bob. "The Cement Ship", *National Motorist*, March-April 1961, p. 15-16.

The Watsonville Register Pajaronian.

Who Was Who in America.

Wig, Rudolph James. "Method of Construction of Concrete Ships," Society of Naval Architects and Marine Engineers, *Transactions*, v. 27, p.1-28, 1919.

Photo Credits

The author and publisher would like to thank those sources which have been forthcoming and generous in their permission to allow their photographs to be reproduced in this book:

Sandy Lydon Collection:	pages 4, 32, 33, 37, 59.
from the Matthews Collection:	pages 31, 36.
Pajaro District Headquarters of the California Department of Parks and Recreation	cover, pages i, xiii, 5, 35, 36, 48, 50, 51, 54, 55, 58, last page.
Library of the National Maritime Museum in San Francisco	pages 17, 19, 20, 23, last page.
Carolyn Swift Collection	back cover, pages 4, 33, 40, 41.
The Harold Van Gorder Collection	pages 21, 26, 48.
Pajaro Valley Historical Association	page 49.
Santa Cruz Sentinel	pages 56, 57.
Register-Pajaronian	page 39.
Bob Smith	page 60.
UCSC Special Collections	pages 38, 45, 51.
UCSC, McHenry Library Map Room	pages 28, 29.
Redwood City Public Library	page 13.
National Archives, Record Group 32 (United States Shipping Board Emergency Fleet Corporation)	page 16.
John A. Campbell	page 24.
Margaret Koch	page 30.
Charles G. Erb	page 34, 44.
Mrs. Creffield	page 50.

Photographs not otherwise cited belong to the author or publisher.

Index

AUTHOR PROFILE

David W. Heron is an Aptos resident with a 36 year long acquaintance of the *S.S.Palo Alto*. Now librarian emeritus from the University of California at Santa Cruz after years of service at university libraries across the U.S. and in Japan, he has written *Night Landing, A Short History of West Coast Smuggling*; has written several articles of a historical nature for professional journals and periodicals; he has also edited a book of essays. He is an active volunteer in several community organizations. David has been known to sail the Bay with friends, albeit on somewhat more conventional craft.

WORLD'S LARGEST CONCRETE TANKER "PALO ALTO" 7,500 TONS D. W. CAPACITY ON DRYDOCK FOR CLEANING, PAINTING AND REPAIRS TO HULL MOORE SHIPBUILDING COMPANY, OAKLAND, CAL., JUNE 16, 1920.   22.01

"Ashes to ashes, dust to dust."

Topics in
Monterey Bay Area History

A series of works that explore specific themes in and around
Santa Cruz and Monterey Counties.

Published by OTTER B BOOKS:
California Central Coast Railways; Rick Hamman
Lighthouse Point: Illuminating Santa Cruz; Frank Perry
Santa Cruz County, Parade of the Past; Margaret Koch
Californians: Searching for the Golden State; James D. Houston
Holy City: Riker's Roadside Attraction; Betty Lewis
Santa Cat: Behind the Lace Curtains: 1856-1926; Margaret Koch
The History of Pigeon Point Lighthouse; Frank Perry
Watsonville: Memories That Linger, Vol I and Vol. II; Betty Lewis

Distributed by OTTER B BOOKS:
Coast Redwoods: Natural and Cultural History: Sandy Lydon et al
Chinese Gold: Chinese in the Mont. Bay Region; Sandy Lydon
Japanese in the Monterey Bay Region; Sandy Lydon
Santa Cruz County Place Names; Donald T. Clark
Highway 17; Richard Beal
Santa Cruz is in the Heart; Geoffrey Dunn
Surf, Sand, and Streetcars; Charles McCaleb
The Santa Cruz County History Journal, Vols. 2, 3, 4, 5
Santa Cruz Mountains Trail Book; Tom Taber
Animals of the Santa Cruz Mountains; Mountain Parks Foundation
Sempervirens Story: Preserving California's Redwoods; Yaryan, Verardo
Night Landing: A Short History of West Coast Smuggling; David Heron
Monterey County Place Names; Donald T. Clark
Monterey County: A Dramatic Story; Augusta Fink
Above Carmel, Monterey, and Big Sur; Cameron & Gilliam
Lighthouse: Point Pinos, Pacific Grove, California; Jerry McCaffery
Creating Carmel; Harold Gilliam